THEORY CONSTRUCTION SERIES

Building Theory From Existing Work:

Finding Your Contribution

Martha A. Garcia-Murillo

Theory Construction Series: Building Theory from Existing Work: Finding Your Contribution

COVER IMAGE: R. J. Wood. File System. U.S. Patent # 1819666, Issued August 18, 1931.

ISBN: 978-0-9854869-2-1

TABLE OF CONTENTS

1

Introduction

Many academics who have gone through the dissertation process or who have advised doctoral students would agree when I say that the most difficult part of the dissertation process is finding a topic. In general, most young scholars start with very large and ambitious projects and feel overwhelmed by the amount of information, readings and conflicting results they come across as they research. For the most part, we know the area that interests us the most; that is the first criterion for selection. For a large project like this, the topic should be of great interest to us, so that it will hold our attention and motivate us for the time it takes to complete it.

Once a topic has been selected, the general practice is to go to electronic databases and the Internet (the default research tool) to search for, skim through, and download papers and web pages that we find relevant to the topic. With a broad topic, this strategy is likely to lead to hundreds, if not thousands, of articles of all kinds on the subject. This task can be even more daunting when doing interdisciplinary research; searches in various disciplinary databases can lead to yet more dozens of articles to read. At that point, the first and most common thing that we tend to do is to begin to read and take notes, and if we are smart, we will start with papers that do a survey of the field. This will at least provide us with a general idea of what has been written thus far. However, one problem with this approach is that most survey pieces are narrowly focused and may not apply to our research area of interest. In the worst case, we will begin reading the articles we found in that first search. I have seen students spend several months reading without getting any closer to a feasible research topic. In this early stage of the research, reading complete papers is a waste of time because of one's lack of experience with the field, which makes it difficult to identify the best or more relevant papers.

A common problem for us researchers is that we are attracted to a multiplicity of ideas, which gets us excited. As we read, we begin to acquire more, not fewer, ideas. Also, after much time spent with individual articles, we may soon find that our idea has already been researched at length. At that point, we tend to get discouraged and start looking for another idea. This, of course, leads to a cycle of attempts where we start the reading process again on a new topic, until we find that it, too, has been heavily investigated. This process is time-consuming and potentially quite discouraging, and it is exacerbated for students who are already quite anxious about finishing the degree and moving on to their future job. Time wasted is not only problematic to the process: it is problematic for a person's mental state because it lengthens the time it takes to finish the degree.

So how can this process be improved to help reduce some of the time that it takes to write a paper or dissertation, and also, potentially, reduce some of the anxiety that it takes to finish this seemingly daunting task? The following sections present some techniques and tools that can make this process more manageable.

The objective of this text is not to guide you on how to do a search (I assume that you already know how to work with databases), but instead to help you identify the holes and/or contradictions in a body of knowledge, where you can make a contribution.

2

Developing Theory From The Existing Literature

With an idea in mind, if we wish to make a contribution to theory, we will need to do a more in-depth study of the existing literature. This will require the building of multiple visual maps to find the holes, contradictions or weaknesses in coverage of the topic. This is a process that in previous years required significant work and experience in an area. The problem, nonetheless, is that as we progress professionally, we find ourselves even busier, with little time to read and keep up with developments in our field. However, with a systematic and organized search process and a little bit of creativity, it becomes much less difficult to make a significant contribution.

Building theory from existing work is a process that requires us to have a research question and a good understanding of the existing contributions. A clear research question is important because it focuses the study, and it is then possible to target contributions that directly address the issue at hand. Theory development goes hand in hand with the development of a research question, a task which is treated in greater detail in another text.

In general, developing theory from existing work involves only a small segment of the field. It is thus necessary, before we are able to develop theory, to go through several iterations of the idea generation process that is described below.

As we narrow the focus on our topic, we need to analyze existing work in an organized manner to help us identify the contributions that have been made. The existing literature thus should be organized to helps us determine the different approaches that have been used to explain a phenomenon as well as the weaknesses and strengths of the work done so far. This will helps us find an area where we can make a contribution.

In any research process, we should be able to identify the significant theoretical contributions that come from fields outside of our own. These do not necessarily need to be completely apart from our home discipline.

Literature analyses are fundamental to theory construction; without an understanding of the field and the contributions that previous scholars have made to it, the field cannot progress.

Scholars who have written about theory all recognize that developing theory requires expertise regarding the phenomenon under investigation (Gioia & Pitre, 1990; Lynham, 2002; Torraco, 2002).

Surprisingly, in graduate schools, there are few courses in the curriculum that teach students how to do literature reviews.

For the most part, when researchers conduct a literature review, they already have a research question in mind, and the purpose of the search is simply to find papers/books that relate to the topic of interest.

Literature reviews for theory construction are slightly different in that no research question is set up from the start. In fact, the research question emerges from the literature review through an iterative process that helps us narrow the focus. This is necessary because, when looking for a topic, we start with broad ideas and find it difficult to narrow our work to a manageable research project.

In theory development, the literature review is the most systematic process. Other steps in the theorizing process, in contrast, call for our creativity and imagination.

It should be noted that theoretical works based on literature reviews can be extensive and can exceed a journal article's page limit. In such situations, it may be useful to provide the initial framework in the literature review paper and then develop the theory fully in a subsequent paper.

3

Using Reference Software

Reference software applications are essential research tools that not only help in the writing of a bibliography, but also help to organize the research process itself. Many applications are available, for purchase or as open source, and thus, it will be important to test a few of these tools to find the one that best fits your research needs.

Among the great benefits of bibliographic software are the built in-technical capabilities that allow easy integration with many electronic databases and web pages. This means that citations found through databases can be imported directly into the software and cited later in the paper.

The first step in the research process is to identify academic papers that are relevant to the topic. This search normally starts in databases. A broad topic is likely to result in hundreds of records. From this list, select those that seem relevant—based solely on the name of the paper or the book. In this initial stage, you do not need to be overly discriminating and can select things that you deem to be relevant or interesting. Among these studies, pay particular attention to papers that have done a survey of the field. As pointed out by Fink (2009), in the literature review process, at a highly practical level, the research should filter out all materials that are difficult to get, are in a different language, or come from a totally different area (e.g., you found a paper on networks from the computer science department, when you are interested only in social networks).

According to Fink (2009), the second step is a quality filter, and the purpose of the literature review is to find holes in the contributions that have been made to a field. There are several iterations of the literature review process. In the first iteration, there should be few filters, if any. For example, doing a search on "diffusion of innovation" can lead to thousands of papers. In fact, this search term in the Web of Science database resulted in 2,264 entries. At first glance, managing all of this seems like an impossible task and most of us will dismiss this first attempt and try to narrow the search using more restrictive search terms. While this may yield a more manageable number of entries, we may be missing an opportunity to find "jewels" among papers that come from different perspectives and disciplines. This tends to happen because, in a second attempt, we may start to focus the search process using keywords that are familiar to us or that fall within our scholarly purview. Innovations often come from the outside, and by setting boundaries, particularly disciplinary boundaries, to our inquiry, we may be missing external contributions that can have an important impact on our field. There is an alternative approach to this process and a way to handle a large number of citations without being completely overwhelmed; this is explained in the next section.

4

Visualizing Within Databases

Today's databases have useful features that can make the literature review a fruitful process for theory generation. Articles found in a database are generally classified by subject, and the subjects correspond roughly to scholarly disciplines. For example, the results of a keyword search for "diffusion of innovations" classified the results under the subject categories listed in Figure 1. Visualization of references will enable us to identify seminal papers in particular fields and make it easier to determine what has been written, or not, about a topic. At this point in the analysis of existing academic work, it is easy to determine whether or not an idea has been studied in-depth.

Figure 1. Division of database results by subject area.

In this first iteration, we might focus on disciplines that are more closely related to our home discipline and work with that subset of results. Notice that the subject categories list the subject areas in descending order, based on the number of contributions found for each category. In this initial search on diffusion of innovation, the business literature has the largest number of contributions.

To illustrate other visualization capabilities, I will now focus only on areas related to research that I may want to pursue. Thus, I will ignore anything from the sciences and focus on fields that I am familiar with, which are business, economics, communication, computer science and information systems. When I refine the search to include only those disciplines, I still have 865 results. These abstracts are the first materials for analysis. The coding to be done on these abstracts is simple, but for some of us, it can be intimidating. Downloading just 500 records can generate up to 200 pages of abstracts. This, for anybody, is a large number of records, and it is precisely because of the sheer amount of work that it is now more difficult to build on existing knowledge instead of coming up with something original. Moreover, the great volume of information that is now at our fingertips makes it hard to track it all thoroughly, and many contributions are lost in the ether. This means that we are losing knowledge by our inability to process and review such large numbers of publications. The process that I illustrate below tries to address this problem.

In the first stage of the literature review, we need to categorize the results. We already started this process when we selected only works from what we considered to be the relevant disciplines. It should be noted that theoretical contributions can be made by filling holes in areas that have been unexplored and that we will be able to find through this analysis of abstracts.

When we are dealing with a large number of citations, we can take advantage of visualization tools built into some these electronic databases to help us identify key contributions. In the Web of Science database, there are a couple of tools that can provide some initial data exploration. After doing our initial search, it is possible to see simple visualizations of the results using the analyze results link. These can be done based on different parameters, such as language, publication year, source title, and subject area. Figure 2 shows the analysis of results by subject area.

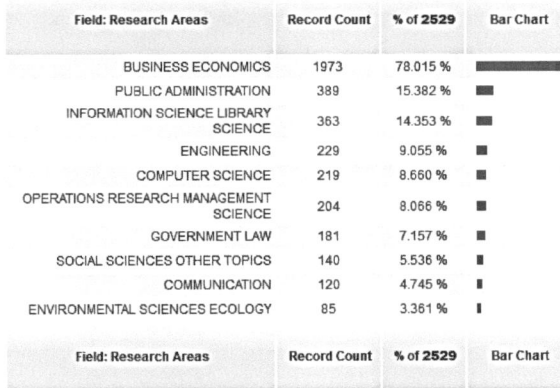

Field: Research Areas	Record Count	% of 2529	Bar Chart
BUSINESS ECONOMICS	1973	78.015 %	
PUBLIC ADMINISTRATION	389	15.382 %	
INFORMATION SCIENCE LIBRARY SCIENCE	363	14.353 %	
ENGINEERING	229	9.055 %	
COMPUTER SCIENCE	219	8.660 %	
OPERATIONS RESEARCH MANAGEMENT SCIENCE	204	8.066 %	
GOVERNMENT LAW	181	7.157 %	
SOCIAL SCIENCES OTHER TOPICS	140	5.536 %	
COMMUNICATION	120	4.745 %	
ENVIRONMENTAL SCIENCES ECOLOGY	85	3.361 %	
Field: Research Areas	Record Count	% of 2529	Bar Chart

Figure 2. Number of contributions by subject area.

Breaking down the citations by subject area is useful for theory building because it helps identify areas where there have been large numbers of contributions. This is important because, even if we are working in an area that differs significantly from our own, we should be aware of the contributions of the field that has generated the most scholarly work. To ignore such a discipline is to miss an important segment of academic work, one that has potentially made the greatest progress on the subject of interest.

It was previously stated that exploring contributions from disciplines far from our home discipline can yield fruitful results. In general, an analysis of contributions from other fields is easy, because the number of works is considerably smaller and doing this can lead to interesting ideas. In this next, second stage of exploration, I selected fields outside my own discipline: nursing, medicine, social work, psychology, mechanics, forestry, thermodynamics and chemistry. This subject selection is to a certain extent arbitrary, because in the research process we are unlikely to be familiar with any of those fields anyway. It is also true that the purpose of reading those works is not to understand the content in detail, but to get a sense of the main idea(s). These foreign ideas could potentially be transferred to my discipline. It is sometimes these transfers of ideas from one field to another that leads to surprising advancements in a field. Figure 3 shows a breakdown by subject of the selected fields.

Field: Research Areas	Record Count	% of 80	Bar Chart
BUSINESS ECONOMICS	76	95.000 %	
ENVIRONMENTAL SCIENCES ECOLOGY	31	38.750 %	
PSYCHOLOGY	22	27.500 %	
HEALTH CARE SCIENCES SERVICES	12	15.000 %	
SOCIAL SCIENCES OTHER TOPICS	11	13.750 %	
URBAN STUDIES	8	10.000 %	
COMMUNICATION	4	5.000 %	
ENERGY FUELS	4	5.000 %	
FOOD SCIENCE TECHNOLOGY	4	5.000 %	
AGRICULTURE	3	3.750 %	
Field: Research Areas	Record Count	% of 80	Bar Chart

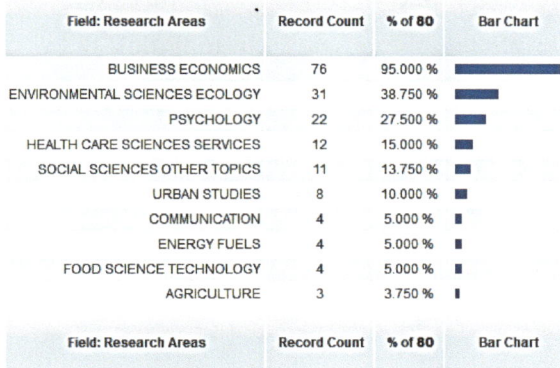

Figure 3. Number of contributions by subject area in fields unrelated to one's discipline.

Outside of business, environmental sciences has had the greatest number of contributions. Scholars in this field, because of the unique challenges they face in taking care our environment, may have found some interesting and unique contributions to our understanding of innovation that can enhance our traditional approach to social sciences and professional disciplines.

When working with fields different from one's own, one way to make the exploration potentially more fruitful is to look at the authors in the list who have published several works, as well as the authors that have been cited the most. You can get this list in the Web of Science database results page by clicking the citation report link. Figure 4 shows the top authors in terms of number of works, and Figure 5shows the most cited. These are good places to start the exploration because those who have been most cited are also more likely to have said something unique to their fields.

Field: Authors	Record Count	% of 1134	Bar Chart
LYYTINEN K	13	1.146 %	I
WATANABE C	11	0.970 %	I
MAHAJAN V	7	0.617 %	I
LAI VS	6	0.529 %	I
RAMAMURTHY K	6	0.529 %	I
AGARWAL R	5	0.441 %	I
CONCEICAO P	5	0.441 %	I
CORROCHER N	5	0.441 %	I
HEITOR MV	5	0.441 %	I
HU MC	5	0.441 %	I
Field: Authors	Record Count	% of 1134	Bar Chart

Figure 4. Main contributors by number of papers published.

Use the checkboxes to remove individual items from this Citation Report or restrict to items published between 1898 and 2012 Go	2008	2009	2010	2011	2012	Total	Average Citations per Year
	2214	2857	2998	3339	1808	20045	393.04
1. Title: User acceptance of information technology: Toward a unified view Author(s): Venkatesh, V; Morris, MG; Davis, GB; et al Source: MIS QUARTERLY Volume: 27 Issue: 3 Pages: 425-478 Published: SEP 2003	226	274	316	310	148	1595	159.50
2. Title: UNDERSTANDING INFORMATION TECHNOLOGY USAGE - A TEST OF COMPETING MODELS Author(s): TAYLOR, S; TODD, PA Source: INFORMATION SYSTEMS RESEARCH Volume: 6 Issue: 2 Pages: 144-176 DOI: 10.1287/isre.6.2.144 Published: JUN 1995	131	147	124	140	55	1043	57.94
3. Title: Information technology adoption across time: A cross-sectional comparison of pre-adoption and post-adoption beliefs Author(s): Karahanna, E; Straub, DW; Chervany, NL Source: MIS QUARTERLY Volume: 23 Issue: 2 Pages: 183-213 DOI: 10.2307/249751 Published: JUN 1999	76	79	71	74	31	526	37.57
4. Title: The process of knowledge transfer: A diachronic analysis of stickiness Author(s): Szulanski, G Source: ORGANIZATIONAL BEHAVIOR AND HUMAN DECISION PROCESSES Volume: 82 Issue: 1 Pages: 9-27 DOI: 10.1006/obhd.2000.2884 Published: MAY 2000	39	37	49	41	18	293	22.54
5. Title: Sectoral systems of innovation and production Author(s): Malerba, F Source: RESEARCH POLICY Volume: 31 Issue: 2 Pages: 247-264 Article Number: PII S0048-7333(01)00139-1 DOI: 10.1016/S0048-7333(01)00139-1 Published: FEB 2002	37	44	24	51	26	258	23.45
6. Title: Models of technology diffusion Author(s): Geroski, PA Source: RESEARCH POLICY Volume: 29 Issue: 4-5 Pages: 603-625 DOI: 10.1016/S0048-7333(99)00092-X Published: APR 2000	27	37	31	35	16	245	18.85
7. Title: The determinants of national innovative capacity Author(s): Furman, JL; Porter, ME; Stern, S Source: RESEARCH POLICY Volume: 31 Issue: 6 Pages: 899-933 Article Number: PII S0048-7333(01)00152-4 DOI: 10.1016/S0048-7333(01)00152-4 Published: AUG 2002	27	37	34	39	12	220	20.00
8. Title: What drives mobile commerce? An empirical evaluation of the revised technology acceptance model Author(s): Wu, JH; Wang, SC Source: INFORMATION & MANAGEMENT Volume: 42 Issue: 5 Pages: 719-729	41	46	30	38	19	205	25.62

Figure 5. Main contributors by number of citations.

This analysis shows that there are authors in these "foreign" fields that should be read because of their apparent impact/importance, given the number of peer citations. In doing this type of exploration, you are indeed in a fishing expedition where the objective, at least of the review of readings outside of your field, is to help you generate ideas that, if modified for your field, could move your home discipline forward.

The objective of this first round of data collection is not necessarily to read to learn, but to get a feeling for the field and to identify significant contributions in other fields that could be modified and appropriated by your own.

When working within our own discipline, a citation analysis often leads to papers that contain extensive and careful reviews of the literature on the topic that we are exploring. These critical reviews are extremely helpful to us academics because they help summarize the field, identify the main contributions, and provide a basis for the field to move forward. A critical literature review on our own topic is a worthwhile effort, not only to help us find the gaps in existing research, but also, if this extensive review is published, to help others to advance the field as well.

As a way of illustrating the potential insights that can be generated from bringing foreign disciplines into our own work, Box 1 shows how Richard Dawkins' work in the field of biology was enriched by bringing religion into his research.

Box 1. Crossing of disciplines

Two independent biologists look at the relationship of the two unlikely discipline partners of biology and religion. Richard Dawkins, from Oxford University, believes that religion is like a disease because it spreads in a similar manner. As he states, in a religion context bits of cultural software take over the hardware of our brain to do irrational things. Corey Fincher, from the University of New Mexico, has a different belief, and thinks not that religion is like a disease but that it is a response to disease. The main idea is not that religion will protect people from diseases, but that such fears may lead to solidarity.

It is from this idea of the relationship between disease and religion that Fincher and his colleague Randy Thornhill began to wonder if disease affects other religion-based behavior. Because diseases can spread more easily when people congregate, they believe that, perhaps in more disease-prone areas, religions will be more exclusive as a way of limiting the number of participants and thus reduce the potential spread of any given disease. To test their hypothesis, they collected information about the number of religions in a country as well as the disease load. The statistical correlation was significant. They report that there is less than one chance in 10,000 that such a relationship would have come about accidentally. Although correlation is not necessarily causation, they also looked at other factors, such as languages. In that study, they found a similar situation. Their argument is that perhaps hostility against a person from another group has nothing to do with the people in the group but the diseases they may bring.

Source: (*The Economist Magazine*, 2008)

5

Visualizing Outside Of Databases

When the abstracts have been identified, they can be organized, classified, and visualized. It is also important to realize that, in many circumstances, this process of reading and categorizing abstracts may have to be repeated, as you begin to find the gaps in the field. This process will also help us identify terms for subsequent searches. The iterative nature of searching and coding from abstracts helps to narrow the focus of the original topic.

The coding and organizing of references provides a bird's-eye view of the field. It also serves to identify the several disciplinary and methodological approaches that have been done before, as well as gaps in research coverage.

In addition to the visualization tools available in databases, there are other visualization tools that can help the process of discovery. This section focuses on the Many Eyes visualization tools because of the many options that are available with that software and because the software is freely accessible on the Internet.

To illustrate the power of visualization, I will use mapped references for the topic "open source communities." Before the references can be entered into ManyEyes, some preliminary work needs to be done.

First, you need to save the relevant abstracts in a reference software application. From these abstracts, you will be making a map of the field in a spreadsheet, a process that I call the *literature review map*. This process requires reading all the abstracts, collecting the data for organizing and analyzing them, coding the information and formatting it in a table. The codes should include, as a minimum, the author, the year, the dependent variable, the independent variable, the theory used, the methodology, the discipline and sub-discipline, and the level of analysis. Figure 6 shows the custom fields that were created within EndNote reference software to collect this data from the abstracts of the initial search. Not all reference software has these capabilities, but a similar set of codes can be created using a spreadsheet.

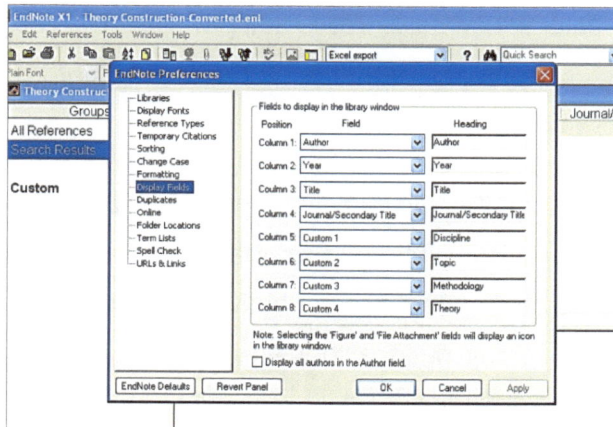

Figure 6. Coding within reference software.

Once you have coded all the abstracts, you can then download them into a spreadsheet. This is necessary because a tree visualization tool requires that the data be formatted in a certain way. Figure 6 shows how generic codes were renamed to input the coding information needed to identify both methodological and disciplinary gaps in existing contributions.

The codes are, to a certain extent, a simplified version of the abstracts, but they allow for better organization of the information.

The discipline code allows us to categorize the source material by discipline, which helps us recognize which ones have made the greatest number of contributions to a topic. In addition this process will help in writing the literature review, having this information will allow us to organize the information by discipline, for example.

Once the coding of the articles has been done, the information can be imported into visualization the software. In our example, the coding was done in EndNote, and the results were then exported to MS Excel, using a custom-made style within EndNote that included only the codes of interest. If the reference software does not allow for the creation of custom fields you can do the coding directly into a spreadsheet. Once the data was in Excel, it was copied and pasted into a three visualization software.

Figures 7, 8 and 9 show three different types of visualizations that are possible with this type of software. We focus on only a few, those which are the most useful for contributing to theory.

Figure 7. Tree map visualization of references.

Figure 8. Tag cloud visualization of references.

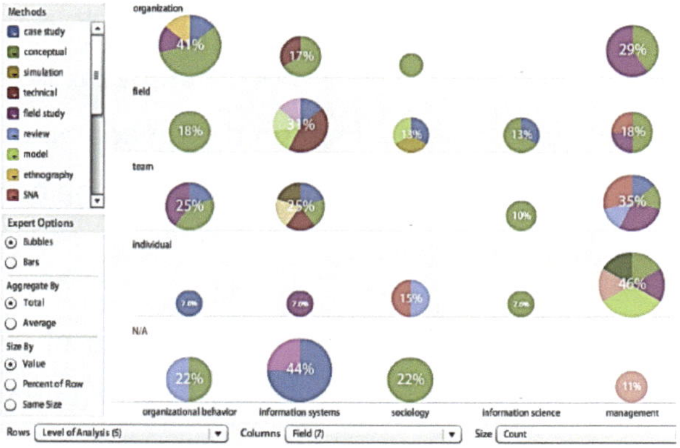

Figure 9. Matrix chart visualization of references.

All of these visualizations can be manipulated to help you find gaps in the literature.

In both figures 7 and 10, there are seven block arrows at the top of the screen shot; these represent the codes that were used to classify the abstracts. The first arrow represents the largest category by which the visualization was organized. In figure 7, the references were first organized by level of analysis, while in figure 10, they were organized by field. The colors represent the different disciplines: management (blue), information systems (yellow), organizational behavior (orange),sociology (green) information science (teal), and human-computer interaction (purple). It is clear from this representation of the references that the fields of research that have contributed the most to the open source research are management information systems and organizational behavior. Thus, when writing about the topic, you should not ignore these fields, and in fact, you should take a closer look at the literature there, to determine the type of contribution that you can make, given their gaps.

The second arrow at the top of the screen shot in figure 10 is Methods. This means that the references organized by fields are then organized by methods. You should notice that within each of the colored fields, grey lines separate the different methods used. For example, for the yellow segment that represents the information systems literature, the papers to the right of the vertical grey line are case studies. Each of the papers within the thicker gray lines represents a different methodology. The last set of lines, the white lines that divide the fields, represent levels of analysis. The papers in this case were coded into four levels: individual, team, organizational, and industry. We can continue the exploration of the literature by continuing to move the arrows, each of which will provide a different

Figure 10. Tree map visualization of references by field.

From this visualization, we note that contributions from management have been the most prolific for the open source field. Most of these were field studies; only one was a grounded theory contribution. As expected, most of the studies were done at the organizational, team, and individual levels; only one used a mixed methods approach.

Because the management literature has made the greatest number of contributions to the open source research field, it is necessary to do a more detailed examination of the management literature. Figure 11 shows two different visualizations of the management contributions: one by method and the other by level. At this point, we can add references from the management literature to get a richer picture of that field and to make sure that no significant contributions have been missed. As can be seen, zooming in on one single field of the visualization provides us with greater detail, such as the level, and the methods used.

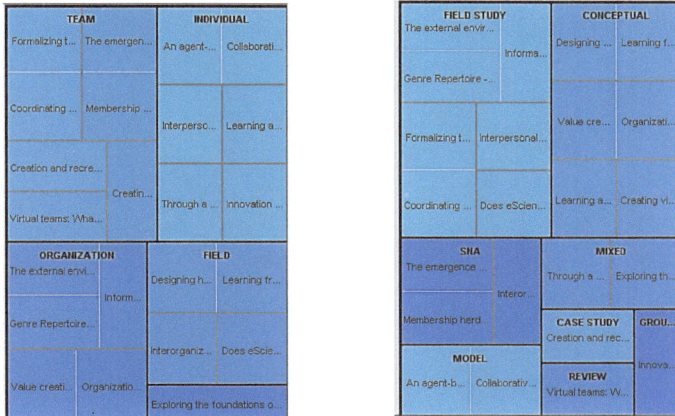

Figure 11. Tree map zoom visualization of references in a single discipline.

The final visualization presented in this text, a matrix, allows coded information to be organized by three different types of codes. Figure 12 shows the same bibliographic information organized in three ways: by theme/topic (rows), level of analysis (columns), and methodology (colors)

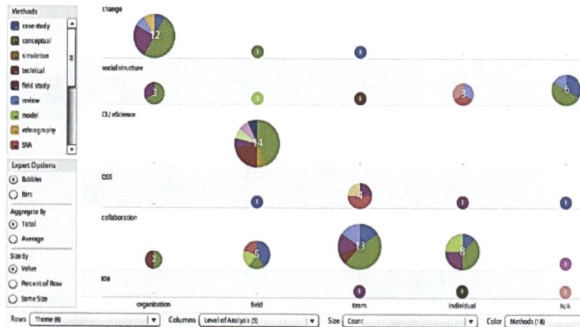

Figure 12. Matrix visualization of references by topic, level, and method.

In this visualization you also have the option to reorganize the columns, rows and pie charts in ways that will help us understand the contributions better.

If in doing this analysis we find a gap, it might be that we did not search enough or collect enough references with abstracts on that particular subject. Thus, again, this prompts the need to go through the abstract organization process to determine if the gap is actually there, or if there is an oversight. Of course, once a gap has been found, you have to ask ourselves if it is there because scholars have failed to recognize the problem or because the issue is not important or interesting. This will help determine if a particular gap is important to address.

Box 2 provides an example of the literature review analysis that was done after the references were analyzed and visualized.

Box 2. Free/Libre Open Source Software

"The literature on success in FLOSS development represented research from several fields, but primarily from software engineering and information systems. The primary research methods used in these studies were case studies, followed by surveys.

Much of the research to date focuses on processes in FLOSS projects, which are readily apparent from the electronic archives of communications available for most projects, though some studies also examine other project characteristics for indications of success factors. Very few studies seem to incorporate both variance and process forms of theory, where theoretical frameworks are used at all.

After inductively coding dozens of articles selected for relevance to the concept of 'success,' the top-level categories of people, product, and process are employed to structure the remaining discussion of the literature."

(Wiggins, 2008)

After having read, coded and visualized abstracts of source materials, we should now be able to identify which fields have contributed the most to your topic, and the main contributors in each of the key fields. This should also help us determine the most common methodological tools used in the topic of interest, as well as the level of analysis. Knowing this makes it easier to discover topics and methodological approaches that have been ignored or are under-researched. An analysis of fields outside of our own discipline can also help us identify ideas that can be appropriated and potentially make an interesting contribution.

Summary

- Finding a contribution to your field requires an understanding of previous work.

- To find research gaps and interesting ideas in other fields, we need to read, code and visualize abstracts of the relevant literature.

- A systematic review will eliminate random searches, which take time and do not assure that important documents have not been missed.

- Visualization tools in databases can help to identify major contributors and contributions.

- Visualization of the literature can reveal disciplinary, methodological and level of analysis gaps, where we can then make a contribution.

References

Fink, A. (2009). *Conducting research literature reviews: from the Internet to paper.* Sage Publications, Inc.

Gioia, D. A., & Pitre, E. (1990). Multiple perspectives on theory building. *Academy of Management Review, 15*(4), 584-602.

Lynham, S. (2002). The general method of applied theory building research. *Advances in Developing Human Resources, 4*(3), 221-241.

The Economist Magazine. (2008). Religion, disease and evolution: Praying for health Retrieved March 18, 2008, from http://www.economist.com/science/displaystory.cfm?story_id=11839270

Torraco, R. J. (2002). Research methods for theory building in applied disciplines: A comparative analysis. *Advances in Developing Human Resources, 4*(3), 355-355.

Wiggins, A. K. (2008). *Theory Construction class paper.* Theory Construction class paper. Syracuse University. Syracuse.

www.ingramcontent.com/pod-product-compliance
Lightning Source LLC
Chambersburg PA
CBHW041224270326
41933CB00001B/33